TheDevilsofLoudun

Edmund Goldsmid

INTRODUCTION

THE following extraordinary account of the *"Cause Célèbre"* of Urbain Grandier, the *Curé* of Loudun, accused of Magic and of having caused the Nuns of the Convent of Saint Ursula to be possessed of devils, is written by an eye-witness, and not only an eyewitness but an actor in the scenes he describes. It is printed at *"Poitiers, chez J. Thoreau et la veuve Ménier, Imprimeurs du Roi et de l'Université 1634."* I believe two copies only are known: my own, and the one in the National Library, Paris. The writer is Monsieur des Niau, Counsellor at la Flèche, evidently a firm believer in the absurd charges brought against Grandier.

Magic appears to have had its origin on the plains of Assyria, and the worship of the stars was the creed of those pastoral tribes who, pouring down from the mountains of Kurdistan into the wide level where Babylon afterwards raised its thousand towers, founded the sacerdotal race of the *Chasdim* or *Chaldeans.* To these men were soon alloted peculiar privileges and ascribed peculiar attributes, until, under the name of Magi, they acquired a vast and permanent influence. Their temples were astronomical observatories as well as holy places; and the legendary tower of Babel, in the Book of Genesis, is probably but the mythical equivalent of a vast edifice consecrated to the study of the seven planets, or perhaps, as the *Bab* (court or palace) of *Bel,* to the brilliant star of good fortune alone. Availing themselves of the general adoration of the stars, they appear to have invented a system of astrology—the apotelesmatic science—by which they professed to decide upon the nature of coming events and the complexion of individual fortunes, with especial reference to the planetary aspects.

In Persia magic assumed a yet more definite development. The Chaldeans had attributed the origin of all things to a great central everlasting fire. The foundation of the Persian system, usually ascribed to Zerdusht or Zoroaster, was the existence of two antagonistic principles—Ormuzd, the principle of good, and Ahriman, the principle of evil. In Persia everything associated with science or religion was included under the denomination "magic." The Persian priests were named the Magnise or Magi, but they did not arrogate to themselves the entire credit of intercourse with the gods. Zoroaster, who was King of Bactria, made some reservations for the sake of exalting the regal power, and taught that the kings were illuminated by a celestial fire which emanated from Ormuzd. Hence the sacred fire always preceded the monarch as a symbol of his illustrious rank; and Plato says the Persian kings studied magic, which is a worship of their gods.

It was, however, in Egypt, that magic received its development as an art. The most famous temples in Egypt were those of Isis, at Memphis and Busiris; of Serapis, at Canopus, Alexandria, and Thebes; of Osiris, of Apis, and Phtha. Isis, the wife of Osiris, derives her name from the Coptic word *isi*, or plenty, and would seem to typify the earth; but she is usually represented as the goddess of the moon (Gr. *kerasphôros*, the horn-bearing). Isis was also employed as a personification of wisdom, and to a certain extent she may be regarded as a symbol of the eternal will, her shrines bearing the enigmatic inscription—"I am the all that was, that is, that will be; no mortal can raise my veil." Horus was the son of Isis, and was instructed by his mother in the art of healing. Horus, synonymous with light, is the king or spirit of the sun. Astrological science and magic were earnestly and eagerly studied by the Egyptian priests. It was their belief that the different stars exercised a powerful influence on the human body. Their funeral ceremonies may be quoted as an illustration, for they agree in sharing among the divinities the entire body of the dead. To Ra, or the Sun, they assigned the head; to Anubis, the nose and lips; to Hathor, the eyes; to Selk, the teeth; and so on. To ascertain the nativity the astrologer had only to combine the theory of the influences thus exercised by these star-related gods with the aspect of the heavens at the moment of an individual's birth. It was an element of the Egyptian as well as of the Persian astrological doctrine that a particular star controlled the natal hour of everyone.[1]

Through the instrumentality of Orpheus, Musæus, Pythagoras, and others, who had travelled in Egypt, and been initiated by the priests into their mysteries, magic found its way into Greece, and there assumed various novel developments. The Greek sorcery was chiefly manifested in the peculiar rites of the Orpheotelesta, the invocation of the dead, the cave of Trophônios, the oracles of the gods, and the worship of Hekatê. The latter mysterious deity, the moon-goddess, was the patron divinity of the sorcerers. From her, as from one of the powers of the nether world, proceeded phantoms that taught witchcraft, hovered among the tombs, and haunted crossways and places accursed by the blood of the murdered or the suicide. "The Mormô, the Cereops, the Empusa, were among the goblin crew that did her bidding."

Rome borrowed her magic, no less than her art and literature, from poetic Hellas. The occult science does not appear to have been known to the Romans until about zoo years before the Christian era. But they had previously cultivated a modification of the Etruscan sorcery, comprising the divination of the future, the worship of the dead, the evocation of their *lemures* or phantoms, and the mystic ceremonies of the Mana-Genita, a nocturnal goddess of awful character. Numa was the great teacher of the ancient Roman magic, which probably partook both of a religious and medical character.

The Christian church, at the outset of its history, forbade the practice of pagan magic, but taught what may be described as a magic of its own. Both Origen and Tertullian held that mania and epilepsy were produced by the action of demons or evil spirits confined within the bodies of the sufferers, and that these were to be exorcised by certain forms of words. The church formally recognized the efficacy of exorcism in 367, when the Council of Laodicea ordained that only those should practise it who were duly authorized by the bishops. Connected with magic and magical rites were the supposed curative properties of the relics of saints, and the divine origin popularly ascribed to visions and ecstatic trances.

In the middle ages magic asserted its supremacy over the whole of Christian Europe; but it had entirely lost the religious character communicated to it by the Chaldeans. It had degenerated into the "black art." It dealt only with the night-side of nature, with the Evil One and his imps, with the loathsome practises of witchcraft and the enchantments of the necromancer. The scholar rose superior to this low kind of theurgy, but he, too, no longer sought communion with the heavenly powers; he devoted all his energies to the discovery of the philosopher's stone and the elixir of eternal youth, to the sources of illimitable wealth andendlesslife . [*Encyc.Nat.* ix. p . 52].

Born at Rouvère, near Sablé, at the very end of the sixteenth century, Urbain Grandier was curate and Canon of Loudun. On obtaining this living, he became so popular a preacher that the envy of the monks was excited against him. Ile was first accused of incontinency; but, being acquitted, his enemies instigated some nuns to play the part of persons possessed, and in their convulsions to charge Grandier with being the cause of their visitation. This horrible, though absurd, charge was countenanced by Cardinal Richelieu, who had been persuaded that Grandier had satirized him. It is this celebrated case which our credulous author here endeavours to prove.

The reader will, no doubt, he interested in the wonderful effects said to have been produced by exorcism. This word is a term applied to the act of driving an evil spirit out of one possessed, by a command in the name of some divine power. The ability to effect this by such means has been accepted as a belief by pagans, Jews, and Christians, and ceremonials with this object are still in use among the Roman Catholics and the closer followers of the teachings of Luther, who continued to keep his opinions in this respect after the Reformation. One of the minor orders of the Roman Catholic clergy exercise the function, and it is only used in cases of supposed demoniacal possession, in the administration of baptism, and in the blessing of the holy oil or *chrism*, and of holy water. [*Nat.Encyc.* v ., p. 389].

"Is not my word like as a fire? saith the Lord; and like a hammer that breaketh the rock in pieces?" (Jer. xxiii. 29).

"Healing by words, that is by the direct expression of the mental power," says Van Helmont, "was common in the early ages, particularly in the church, and not only used against the devil and magic arts, but also against all diseases. As it commenced in Christ, so will it continue for ever." (Operatio sanandi a primordio fuit in ecclesia per verbs, ritus, exorcismos, aquam, panem, salem, herbas, idque nedum contra diabolos et effectus magicos, sed et morbos omnes. *Opera omnia, de virtute magna verborum et rerum*, p. 753). Not only did the early Christians heal by words, but the old magicians performed their wonders by magic formulas. "Many cures," says the Zendavesta, "are performed by herbs and trees, others by water, and again others by words; for it is by means of the divine word that the sick are the most surely healed." The Egyptians also believed in the magic power of words. Plotin cured Porphyrius, who lay dangerously ill in Sicily, by wonder-working words; and the latter healed the sick by words, and cast out the devil by exorcism. The Greeks were also well acquainted with the power of words, and give frequent testimony of this knowledge in their poems; in the oracles, exhortation and prayer were universal. Orpheus calmed the storm by his song; and Ulysses stopped the bleeding of wounds by the use of certain words. Among the Greeks, healing by words was so common that in Athens it was strictly forbidden. A woman was even stoned for using them, as they said that the gods had given healing virtues to stones, plants, and animals, but not to words (Leonard. Varius de fascino, Paris, 1587, lib. ii. p. 147). Cato is said to have cured sprains by certain words. According to Pliny, he did not alone use the barbaric words "motas, daries, dardaries, astaries," but also a green branch, four or five feet long, which he split in two, and caused to be held over the injured limb by two men. Marcus Varro, it is said, cured tumours by words. Servilius Novianus cured affections of the eyes by causing an inscription to be worn suspended round the neck, consisting of the letters *A* and *Z;* but the greatest celebrity was gained by Serenus Sammonicus by his wonder-working hieroglyphics. They were supposed to be a certain cure for fever, and were in the subjoined form:—

A B R A C A D A B R A

B R A C A D A B R

R A C A D A B

A C A D A

A

Talismans were inscribed with various signs; and many customs still in use in the East originate from them. Angerius Fererius, in his "Vera medendi methodus, lib. ii. c. ii. de homerica medicatione," speaks very plainly on this subject: "Songs and characters have not alone this power: it exists also in a believing mind, which is produced in the unlearned by the help of visible signs, and in the learned by an acknowledged and peculiar influence." (Non sunt carmina, non characteres, qui talia possunt, sed vis animi confidentis, et cum patiente concordis, ut doctissime a poeta dictum sit:

Nos habitat, non Tartara, sed nec sidera cœli;
Spiritus in nobis qui viget, illa facit.

Doctis et rerum intelligentiam habentibus, nihil opus est externis, sed cognita vi animi, per eam miracula edere possunt. Indoctus ergo animus, hoc est, suæ potestatis et naturæ inscius, per externa illa confirmatus, morbos curare poterit. Doctus vero et sibi constans, solo verbo sanabit; aut ut simul intactum animum afficiat, externa quoque assumet.)

The living Word, which illuminated mankind through Christ, showed its divine power over disease; and the true followers of Christ can perform wonders by the power of his word. "Etenim sanatio in Christo Domino incœpit," says Helmont, "per apostolos continuavit et modo est, atque perennis permanet."—Our Lord said to the sick man, Arise and walk; and he arose and went his way: open thine eyes; and he saw: take up thy bed and walk; and he stood up; Lazarus, come forth! and he that was dead came forth, bound hand and foot with grave-clothes, and his face was bound about with a napkin, &c. But what is this word, which is sharper than a two-edged sword? It is the Divine spirit, which is ever present, ever active; it is the Divine breath which inspires man. In all ages, and in every nation, there have been men who possessed miraculous powers; but they were inspired by religion—turned towards God in prayer and unity. The Almighty sees the heart of the supplicant, and not alone their words; he sees the belief and intention, and not the rank or education.

Even the pious heathens prayed to God; and their peculiar worship maintained the connection, and brought about a still closer union, between individuals and God, and enabled them, in some measure, to pierce the veil of ignorance and darkness. And the pious heathen endeavoured with all his energies to raise himself to a more intimate relation with God, and, therefore, a peculiar force lay in the means employed; and what could be more powerful than prayer? and God, in his comprehensive love and affection, would not leave, these supplicants unanswered.

It would be superfluous to enumerate many instances of the efficacy of prayer, as exemplified in pious and believing men, which we might meet with in all ages, and among all nations. In later times many are well known. I shall, however, mention one, which appears to me the clearest and least doubtful. Kiersen relates as follows: "I knew a seer who gained a power of foretelling the future by prayer during the night on a mountain, where he was accustomed to lie on his face; and he used this power for the assistance of the sick in the most unpretending manner. His visions are partly prosaic, partly poetical, and have reference not only to sickness, but also to other important, and even political, events, so that he has much resemblance to the prophets of the Old Testament."

For those to whom the universe is a piece of clockwork, or a perpetual motion, which continues moving for ever of its own accord—to whom the everlasting power and wisdom and love in eternity and nature is as nothing, prayer and supplication must seem objectless and insipid; but they will never be able to perform the works of the soul. To these, the magical effects are just as inexplicable (and, therefore, untrue) as the magical phenomena are unknown. But, with all their knowledge and wisdom of the world, nature will ever remain to them a mystery.

This is not the place to enter more fully into this subject; but it may not be superfluous to remember that in every word there is a magical influence, and that each word is in itself the breath of the internal and moving spirit. A word of love, of comfort, of promise, is able to strengthen the timid, the weak, or the physically ill; but words of hatred, censure, enmity. or menace, lower our confidence and self-reliance. How easily the worldling, who rejoices under good fortune, is cast down under adversity, and despair only enters where religion is not—where the mind has no inward and divine comforter. But there is, probably, no one who is proof against curse or blessing. [Ennemoser, *Hist.ofMagic* , I., p. 120.]

PART 1

AT the beginning of the 17th century, the curate of Loudun was Urbain Grandier. To those talents which lead to success in this world, this man united a corruption of morals which dishonoured his character. His conduct had made him many enemies. These were not merely rivals, but husbands and fathers, some of high position, who were outraged at the dishonour he brought on their family. He was, nevertheless, a wonderfully proud man, and the bitterness of his tongue and the harshness with which he pursued his advantages only excited them the more. And these advantages were numerous, for he had a marvelous faculty for pettifogging. His iniquities had rendered him the scourge of the town, whose principal curate and greatest scandal he was at one and the same moment. This is proved by the dispensations obtained by many fathers of families to assist at the divine service in some other parish, and by the permissions granted them to receive the sacrament from some other hand.[2]

But what was still more serious is, that while setting so many people against him, he had been able to form as formidable a party of his own. These were almost all Huguenots,[3] of which Loudun was then full. He had gained their good graces so much that they upheld him to the utmost of their power. This gave rise to the suspicion that he was merely a disguised Calvinist; a by no means unusual occurrence. Thus Grandier, believing himself safe, put no bounds to his audacity. He treated those from whom he differed with contempt, and in his preachings even dared to question the privileges of the Carmelites. He publicly ridiculed their sermons. He even encroached on episcopal jurisdiction, by granting dispensations from the publication of marriage banns. This last act caused a sensation, and was reported to Louis de la Rocheposay, Bishop of Poitiers, to whom, at the same time, were addressed numerous complaints of the irregular conduct of the curate and of the scandal he caused. The prelate had him arrested, and imprisoned till his trial, which took place on the 2nd June 1630, when he was condemned to fast on bread and water every Friday for three months, forbidden to officiate in the diocese for five years, and interdicted for all time from performing divine service in the town of Loudun. Grandier appealed against this sentence to the Metropolitan, M. d'Escoubleau de Sourdis, Archbishop of Bordeaux, and since then created Cardinal; and the prosecution appealed to the parliament of Paris against this attempt to evade the jurisdiction of the Bishop. But as many witnesses had to be heard, most of whom lived in the diocese, the parliament remitted the case to the Courts of Poitiers. Grandier was thus enabled to face his adversaries, thanks to the friends he had in the district. The following fact proves this.

Amongst other witnesses, two priests, Gervais Méchin, and Louis Boulieau deposed that they had found Grandier lying with women and girls flat on the ground in his Church, the gates leading to the street being shut; that several times, at extraordinary hours, both during the day and during the night they had seen women and girls come to his room; that some remained there from one o'clock its the afternoon, till past midnight, and had their suppers brought there by their maidservants; who used to withdraw at once; that they had also seen him in his Church, with the doors wide open, and, that some women having entered, they were at once closed.

Such evidence was absolute ruin to Grandier consequently his friends moved heaven and earth. They used bribery and threats against these priests, and obtained from them a retractation of their evidence. René Grandier, brother of the accused, wrote it with his own hand, as was afterwards proved, and the two priests signed it. This evidence destroyed, the cabal had little trouble in turning the legal proceedings to the advantage of Grandier. The Court of Poitiers pronounced his acquittal of the charges brought against him. He was so triumphant, that he insulted his enemies and treated them with public contempt, as if he were entirely 'out of the wood,' He had yet to appear before the tribunal of the Archbishop of Bordeaux, to whom he had appealed. But here again his friends stood by him, and he obtained a second acquittal and an order reinstating him in all his functions (22nd Nov. 1631). The verdict contained a warning to him "to behave well and decently, according to the Holy Decretals and Canonical Constitutions."

At the same time, the Archbishop, in slew of the animosity of his adversaries, thought it would be better and safer for him to exchange livings; and he advised him to leave a town where he was looked upon with such disfavour.

Grandier did not think proper to follow the advice or obey the order: far from showing the modesty which was enjoined him, he looked upon his acquittal as a triumph, and returned to Loudun with a laurel branch in his hand, for the mere purpose of insulting his opponents.

Neutral persons were shocked at so little modesty of conduct, his enemies were irritated, and even his friends blamed him. Without pausing an instant he set to work to obtain every advantage over his adversaries. He was not satisfied with having obtained the full mead he was entitled to; he resolved to carry his vengeance as far as law would allow him; and prepared to prosecute before the Courts all those who had taken steps against him, and to claim damages of various amounts, and the restitution of the revenues of his cure, the sentence of the Archbishop. of Bordeaux entitling him thereto. In vain did his best friends use every means to turn him Iron so imprudent a design: God, who intended to cut off this gangrenous member from the body of His Church, and to make of him an example memorable to all ages, abandoned him to his own wilful blindness. Nevertheless, amidst all these proceedings, nothing had been as yet heard of Magic, and up to this time no one had even thought of suspecting him of that crime.

Six years previously, a convent of nuns of the order of St. Ursula had established itself at Loudun. This community, like every new institution, was in somewhat straitened circumstances; though the social position of its members was good. Most of them were daughters of the nobility, while the remainder belonged to the best "Bourgeoisie" of the country. The good reputation of the new order (it was not quite fifty years old), and the high character it bore in Loudun, had also attracted to it a great number of pupils. The nuns were therefore enabled, with economy, to make ends meet, and could look forward to the future with confidence.

The Mother Superior, Madame de Belfiel, daughter of the Marquis de Cose, was related to M. de Laubardemont, Counsellor of State and afterwards Intendent of the provinces of Touraine, Anjou, and Maine. Madame de Sazilli was a connection of the Cardinal de Richelieu. The two ladies de Barbesiers, sisters, belonged to the house of Nogeret. Madame de la Mothe was daughter of the Marquis de la Motte Baracé in Anjou. There was also a Madame d'Escoubleau , of the same name and family as the Archbishop of Bordeaux. Thus they could flatter themselves with dreams of future successes, when they happened to lose their Prior Moussaut, who had charge of their spiritual welfare.

A successor had now to be sought. Grandier, who had never had any connection with the convent, offered himself nevertheless as a candidate. The proposal was scornfully rejected; and the Superior, Madame de Belfiel, had a great quarrel with one of her friends, who urged her to appoint this priest. The choice of the convent fell on Canon Mignon, a man of considerable merit, and in whom spiritual gifts were only equalled by intellectual ones. Grandier, already irritated at his own want of success, was still more annoyed at Mignon's appointment. The contrast in all points between his character and that of the Canon was too great for any other result to have been looked for. Every honest man takes a pride in the blamelessness of his profession, and cannot look favourably on a colleague who dishonours it, nor speak favourably of him. The curate, then, had nothing to expect from the Canon, who was very intimate with the Bishop,[4] and he had already been made aware of the opinions Mignon had expressed at the time of the first trial. These circumstances were not likely to induce Grandier to look with a kindly eye on his successful competitor, and he consequently determined to give plenty of work to the confessor and to his penitents.

Of the various functions the priest is called upon to perform, none requires such delicacy of treatment as the ministry of the tribunal of Penitence.[5] It becomes still more delicate where the consciences of nuns are concerned. But the burden is intolerable, and few could bear it, if extraordinary agencies are employed to increase the difficulty. The anxiety of a newly-appointed confessor in such a situation would be easily understood by Grandier, and would tend to console him for his failure in obtaining the coveted position.

However this may be, extraordinary symptoms began to declare themselves within the convent, but they were hushed up as far as possible, and not allowed to be known outside the walls. To do otherwise would have been to give the new institution a severe blow, and to risk ruining it at its birth. This the nuns and their confessor understood. It was therefore decided to work in the greatest secrecy, and to cure, or at least mitigate, the evil.

It was hoped that God, touched by the patience with which the chastisement was borne, would Himself, in His mercy, send a remedy.

That was all that prudence could devise, but *human* prudence, always infinitely limited in its views; *Divine* prudence is quite another thing. God had resolved that the mystery of iniquity should no longer lie buried. As the church, at its birth, gained great credit through similar events,[6] so again, in this case, did they serve to revive the faith of true believers, end so it will be again in future times.

Loudun was fated to behold events of this nature, and they were to produce their ordinary effect, viz., to enlighten those whose consciences, though distorted, had preserved some remnants of original good, and to blind souls darkened with pride, and hearts full of perversity.

As usually happens, the extraordinary phenomena displayed in the persons of the nuns were taken for the effects of sexual disease. But soon suspicions arose that they proceeded from supernatural causes; and at last they perceived what God intended every one to see.

Thus the nuns, after having employed the physicians of the body, apothecaries and medical men, were obliged to have recourse to the physicians of the soul, and to call in both lay and clerical doctors, their confessor no longer being equal to the immensity of the labour. For they were seventeen in number; and everyone was found to be either fully possessed, or partially under the influence of the Evil One.

All this could not take place without some rumours spreading abroad; vague suspicions floated through the city; had the secret even been kept by the nuns, their small means would soon have been exhausted by the extraordinary expenses they were put to in trying to hide their affliction, and this, together with the number of people employed in relieving them, must have made the matter more or less public. But their trials were soon increased when the public was at last made acquainted with their state. The fact that they were possessed of devils drove everyone from their convent as from a diabolical residence, or as if their misfortune involved their abandonment by God and man. Even those who acted thus were their best friends. Others looked upon these women as mad, and upon those who tended them as visionaries. For, in the beginning, people being still calm, had not come to accuse them of being imposters.

Their pupils were first taken from them; most of their relations discarded them; and they found themselves in the deepest poverty. Amidst the most horrible vexations of the invisible spirit, they were forced to labour with their hands, to earn their bread. What was most admirable was that the rule of the community was never broken. Never were they known to discontinue their religious observances, nor was divine service ever interrupted. Ever united, they retained unbroken the bonds of charity which bound them together. Their courage never failed, and when the seizure was past, they used to return to their work or attend the services of the Church with the same modesty and calmness as in the happy days of yore. I know that malice will not be pleased at such a pleasing portraiture. But this base feeling, too natural in the human heart, should be banished thence by all men of honour, who know its injustice and only require that history should be truthful. Probability itself is in favour of our statements. For when God permits us to be attacked so violently by our common enemy, it is as a trial to ourselves, to sanctify us and raise us to a high degree of perfection, and simultaneously He prepares us for victory, and grants us extraordinary grace, which we have only to assimilate and profit by.

It became necessary to have recourse to exorcisms. This word alone is for some people a subject of ridicule, as if it had been clearly proved that religion is mere folly and the faith of the church a fable. True Christians must despise these grinning impostors. Exorcisms, then, were employed. The demon, forced to manifest himself, yielded his name. He began by giving these girls the most horrible convulsions; he went so far as to raise from the earth the body of the Superior who was being exorcised, and to reply to secret thoughts, which were manifested neither in words nor by any exterior signs. Questioned according to the form prescribed by the ritual, as to why he had entered the body of the nun, he replied, it was from hatred. But when, being questioned as to the name of the magician, he answered that it was Urbain Grandier, profound astonishment seized Canon Mignon and his assistants. They had indeed looked upon Grandier as a scandalous priest; but never had they imagined that he was guilty of Magic. They were therefore not satisfied with one single questioning: they repeated the interrogatory several times, and always received the same reply.

PART 2

THE declaration of the Evil Spirit could not to make a great commotion, and to have results which required precautions to be taken at once. The Canon, like a wise man, put himself in communication with Justice, and informed the magistrates of what was passing at the convent, on the 11th October, 1632. Grandier, prepared for all contingencies, had already taken his measures. Many of the magistrates belonged to the new religion and were favourable to him, looking upon him as a secret adherent; they served him as he expected. At the same time, he made all possible use of his extraordinary talents for pettifogging, presented petition on petition, questioned every statement of the exorcists and of the nuns, threatened their confessor Mignon, complained that his reputation was attacked, and that the means were thus taken from him of doing the good his position required, and demanded that the nuns should be locked up and the exorcisms be put an end to. He knew well enough that his demands were out of the question, and that civil justice has nothing to do with the exercise of religious functions. But he wished, if possible, to embarrass the exorcists, and commit the judges with the bishops, or, at any rate, throw discord among them, and give his Calvinists an opportunity of crying out; he succeeded.

The magistrates separated. Only those who were favourable to him remained: the rest ceased to appear at the exorcisms, and Mignon soon withdrew from the convent. Excitement rose in the public mind, a thousand arguments on this or that side permeated the town, and a thousand quarrels took place on all sides.

This excitement, however, and these disputes settled nothing, and the exorcisms, which continued, had no better result. Grandier triumphed, and his friends admired his wit, his skill, and proclaimed aloud that he could be convicted of nothing, not even as regards women, although they knew well how far he had gone in this matter. Until now, the Court had taken no notice of the affair; but the noise it had made in the world since the first days of October 1632 had reached the Queen's ears. She requested information, and the Abbé Marescot, one of her chaplains, was sent to examine into the matter and report to her. He arrived at Loudun on the 28th November, and witnessed what was going on. No immediate consequences followed: but an incident soon occurred, which caused a sudden change in the position of affairs.

The King had resolved to raze the castles and fortresses existing in the heart of the kingdom, and commissioned M. de Laubardemont to see to the demolition of that of Loudun. He arrived, and saw what a ferment the town was in, the animosity that reigned there, and the kind of man who caused the commotion. The complaints of those who were victims of the debaucheries, of the pride, or of the vengeance of the curate, touched him, and it seemed to him important to put an end to the scandal. On his return he informed the King and the Cardinal-Minister of the facts: Louis XIII., naturally pious and just, perceived the greatness of the evil, and deemed it his duty to put a stop to it. He appointed M. de Laubardemont to investigate the matter without appeal; with orders to choose in the neighbouring jurisdictions the most straightforward and learned judges. The Commission is dated 30th November, 1633.

Nothing less was needed to bring to justice a man upheld by a seditious and enterprising party, and so well versed in the details of *chicannerie:* an art always shameful in any man, but especially to an ecclesiastic. The King issued at the same time two decrees, to arrest and imprison Grandier and his accomplices. Armed with such powers, the Commissioner did not fear to attack a man who had so often succeeded in gaining either a nonsuit on some question of form, or in turning accusations to his own advantage, or else dragging out proceedings to such a length as to weary his adversaries and his judges.

The Calvinists, already irritated at the razing of the Castle which served them as a rallying place in times of rebellion, cried out against this new tribunal, because they saw that it was the sole means of rendering useless the knaveries of their friend. But they cried out much louder when the Commissioner arrested the accused, without waiting for informations, and seized all his papers. As if it were not well known that, in criminal matters, this mode of proceeding is usual. In this case it was absolutely necessary. For, without this precaution, Grandier might have fled, and defended himself from afar, engaging the attention of judges, who had plenty of work elsewhere. He might even have raised tumults in the city, which might have necessitated violent remedies.

These precautions being taken, the Commissioner commenced his investigation, and proceeded to hear witnesses on the 17th December, 7633.

The Commissioner now learned of what Grandier and his party were capable. The witnesses were so intimidated that none would speak, and it required all the Royal Authority to reassure them. He therefore issued a proclamation forbidding the intimidation of witnesses, under penalty of prosecution; and the Bishop of Poitiers having supported the King's decision, the two priests, Gervais Méchin and Martin Boulieau, who had been forced to retract their evidence in the former trial, presented a petition in which they declared that they had been seduced and constrained by several persons in authority to recall their evidence, and they now affirmed their first evidence to be true. The evidence of the nuns was also heard, and that of lay persons of both sexes, amongst others of two women, the one of whom confessed having had criminal relations with Grandier, and that he had offered to make her Princess of Magicians, whilst the second confirmed the evidence of the first.[7]

As regards the nuns, they deposed that Grandier had introduced himself into the convent by day and night for four months, without anyone knowing how he got in; that he presented himself to them whilst standing at divine service and tempted them to indecent actions both by word and deed; that they were often struck by invisible persons; and that the marks of the blows were so visible that the doctors and surgeons had easily found them, and that the beginning of all these troubles was signalized by the apparition of Prior Moussaut, their first confessor. The Mother Superior and seven or eight other nuns, when confronted with Grandier, identified him, although it was ascertained that they had never seen him save by magic, and that he had never had anything to do with their affairs. The two women formerly mentioned and the two priests maintained the truth of their evidence. In a word, besides the nuns and six lay women, "sixty witnesses deposed to adulteries, incests, sacrileges, and other crimes, committed by the accused, even in the most secret places of his church, as in the vestry, where the Holy Host was kept, on all days and at all hours."

It may well be imagined that the mother, brothers and friends of the accused did not abandon him. They appealed to every possible authority. The details of these proceedings would be as wearisome as useless, as the Commissioner, by the very terms of his Commission, was placed above all such dilatory pettifogging, and therefore refused or annulled all applications in that direction. He then questioned the accused as to the facts and articles of accusation, and after, having made hint sign his confessions and denials, proceeded to Paris to inform the Court of what he had done.

The King and his Council thought it right to furnish him with means to overcome all obstacles to a speedy decision. This precaution was necessary, for letters from the Bailly of Loudun, Grandier's chief supporter, to the Procurator-General of the Parliament, were intercepted, in which it was asserted that the "possession" was an imposter. The latter's reply was also seized. Monsieur de Laubardemont returned therefore to Loudun with a Decree of the Council, dated 31st May 1634, confirming all his powers and *prohibiting Parliament and all other judges from interfering in this business, and forbidding all parties concerned from appealing, under penalty of a fine of five hundred livres.* He caused Grandier to be transferred from the prison of Augers to that of Loudun, so as to have him at hand to confront with witnesses, if need be.

But, first of all, he considered it necessary to examine the nuns carefully; for this purpose, with the consent of the Bishop, he sequestrated them in different convents, and interrogated them so severely that one might have thought that they themselves were the magicians. "He saw them all, the one after the other, for several days; and listened to their conversations, to observe their mode of thought. He enquired minutely into their lives, their morals, their behavior, not only secular but religious. His depositions, or notes, which represented the evidence of twenty girls, including a few not nuns, filled fifty rolls of official paper, and were the admiration of all judges, so great was the prudence and care they demonstrated."

On the other hand the Bishop of Poitiers, after having sent several Doctors of Theology to examine the victims, came to Loudun in person, and exorcised them himself, or had them exorcised by others in his presence for two months and a half. Never was work done with such care and attention.

All precognitions over, the Commissioner began to confront the accused with the witnesses, and the latter maintained, face to face with Grandier, the evidence they had given against him.

As regard the nuns, it was observed that they never contradicted themselves, whether questioned together or separately, though they were examined often, by different persons, and as skilfully as possible. Now, criminals do not manage this, for the cleverest have the greatest difficulty in avoiding contradictory statements. Those writers, who have supported Grandier, have never discovered the least discrepancy in the evidence of the nuns. Nor did Grandier ever plead malice on their part as a defence, for they had never seen him, nor had he had anything to do with their affairs, as we have said.

If, as calumny asserts, the only thing sought was the death of Grandier, here were sufficient proofs to burn him, if only for abusing the privileges of his ministry and of his Church, or for the sacrileges he had committed therein. But justice is not satisfied with punishing one kind of crime, when she finds traces of another still more serious. It was moreover a Christian duty to assist the views of God, who permitted so strange an event, to confound the calumnies of the protestants, and to prove the demonstration the "possession" of the nuns, and the magic exercised by the accused. To this the Commissioners and the other judges applied themselves.

Thus, as it was a matter rather of religion than of jurisprudence, they resolved to begin by prayer to God, who is the Father of all Light, rightly considering that all France was watching the trial with eager eyes, that it was shrouded in a thick veil of obscurity, and that their verdict would entail important consequences. They therefore prepared to receive divine assistance and grace by frequent confessions, and by often receiving the Holy Sacrament. Then they decreed a general procession to implore celestial aid in so difficult a matter; and, to excite the devotion of the masses by their example, they went in a body, during the whole of the trial, to visit the Churches of the city, set aside by the Bishop for forty hour services, and reached each in time for the elevation of the host. Thence the Exorcists went to the Church fixed upon for the Exorcisms, and the judges proceeded to the tribunal to continue the case; in the evening all returned to church for evensong.

The examination lasted forty days, during which Demons gave them the clearest proofs of their presence in the bodies of the persons exorcised, and every day added new evidence against Grandier, and yet never said anything against him which did not turn out strictly true. These assertions merit distinct proof, which will be found interesting.

As regards the presence of Devils in the possessed, the Church teaches us in its ritual, that there are four principal signs, by which it can be undoubtedly recognised. These signs are the speaking or understanding of a language unknown to the person possessed; the revelation of the future, or of events happening far away; the exhibition of strength beyond the years and nature of the actor; and floating in the air for a few moments.

The Church does not require, in order to have recourse to Exorcisms, that all these marks should be found in the same subject; one alone, if well authenticated, is sufficient to demand public exorcism.

Now, they are all to be found in the Nuns of Loudun, and in such numbers that we can only. mention the principal cases.

Acquaintance with unknown tongues first showed itself in the Mother-Superior. At the beginning, she answered in Latin the questions of the Ritual proposed to her in that language. Later, she and the others answered in any language they thought proper to question in.

M. de Launay de Razilli, who had lived in America, attested that, during a visit to Loudun, he had spoken to them in the language of a certain savage tribe of that country, and that they had answered quite correctly, and had revealed to him events that had taken place there.

Some gentlemen of Normandy certified in writing that they had questioned Sister Clara de Sazilli in Turkish, Spanish, and Italian, and that her answers were correct.

M. de Nismes, Doctor of the Sorbonne, and one of the chaplains of the Cardinal de Lyon, having questioned them in Greek and German, was satisfied with their replies in both languages.

Father Vignier, Superior of the Oratory at La Rochelle, bears witness in his Latin Narrative, that, having questioned Sister Elizabeth a whole afternoon in Greek, she always replied correctly and obeyed him in every particular.

The Bishop of Nimes commanded Sister Clara in Greek to raise veil and to kiss the railings at a certain spot; she obeyed, and did many other things he ordered, which caused the prelate to exclaim that one must be an Atheist or lunatic not to believe in "possession."

Some doctors questioned them also as to the meaning of some Greek technical terms, extremely difficult to explain, and only known to the most learned men, and they clearly expressed the real signification of the words.

Lastly, Grandier himself being confronted with them, his Bishop invested him with the stole to exorcise the Mother Superior, who, he declared, knew Latin; but he did not dare to question her or the others in Greek, though they dared him to it; whereon he remained very embarrassed.[8]

As to the Revelation of hidden matters or of events passing afar off, proofs are still more abundant. We will only select a few of the most remarkable.

M. Morin, Prior of St. Jacques de Thouars, having requested M. Morans, Commissioner appointed by the Bishop of Poitiers to watch over the possessed, and to assist in the trial of Grandier, to allow some sign to be given proving *actual infernal possession*, whispered to M. de Morans that he wished one of the possessed to bring him five rose leaves. Sister Clara was then away in the refectory; M. de Morans ordered, in his thoughts, the Demon who possessed her to obey the wish of M. Morin, for the greater glory of God. Thereupon the Nun left the refectory, and went into the garden, whence she brought first a pansy and other plants, and presented them with roars of laughter, saying to M. de Morans: "Is that what you wish, father? I am not a Devil, to guess your thoughts."—To which he replied simply: "*Obedias*," obey. She then returned to the garden, and after several repetitions of the order, presented through the railings a little rose branch, on which were six leaves. The Exorcist said to her: "*Obedias punctualiter sub pœnâ maledictionis*," obey to the letter under penalty of malediction; she then plucked off one leaf, and offered the branch saying: "I see you will only have five; the other was one too many." The Prior was so convinced by what he saw, that he went out with tears in his eyes. An official report of the fact was drawn up.

Madame de Laubardemont also tried the sane experiment, in order to convince many sceptics who were present: and she was equally successful.

The *Liententant-Criminel* of Orle ans, the President Tours, Lieutenant-General de S. Maixant, and myself[9] also had our curiosity gratified. I desired that Sister Clara should bring me her beads, and say an *Ave-Maria*. She first brought e. pin, and then some aniseed; being urged to obey, she said: "I see you want something else," and then she brought me her beads and offered to say an *Ave-Maria*.

M. Chiron, Prior of Maillezais, desiring to strengthen his belief in demoniacal possession, begged M. de Morans to allow him to whisper to a third party the sign he required; and he thereon whispered to M. de Fernaison, Canon and Provost of the same Church, that he wished the nun to fetch a missal then lying near the door, and to put her finger on the introit of the mass of the Holy Virgin, beginning "Salve, Sancta parens." M. de Morans, who had heard nothing, ordered Sister Clara, who was likewise ignorant of what had been said, to obey the intentions of M. Chiron. This young girl then fell into strange convulsions, blaspheming, rolling on the ground, exposing her person in the most indecent manner, without a blush, and with foul and lascivious expressions and actions,[10] till she caused all who looked on to hide their eyes with shame. Though she had never seen the prior, she called him by his name, and said he should be her lover. It was only after many repeated commands, and an hour's struggling, that she took up the missal, saying: "I will pray." Then, turning her eyes in another direction, she placed her finger on the capital S at the beginning of the introit aforesaid, of which facts reports were drawn up.

M. de Milliere, a gentleman of Maine, certified that, being present at the Exorcism of Sister Clara, and on his knees, the Devil asked him whether he was saying a *De Profundis* for his wife, which was the case. The Marquis de la Mothe, son of M. de Parabel, governor of Poitou, certified that sister Louise de Nogeret had disclosed his most secret faults in the presence of Father Tranquille, and of Madame de Neuillant, his aunt.

The same M. de la Mothe also asked an Exorcist to make Sister Clara, who was in the convent, come out, kneel down, and say an Ave Maria; she came after repeated commands, and obeyed.

Chevalier de Mere, who was present, asked the Devil on what day he had last confessed. The Devil answered Friday. The Chevalier acknowledged this to be correct; whereupon Sister Clara withdrew. But as he wished to try the Devil again, he begged the exorcist to make her return, and whispered some words to the Marquis and the Monk, for the nun to repeat. The exorcist refused, as the words were indecent. He changed them, therefore, into *Pater, et Filius et Spiritus Sanctus!* He whispered these words so low, that the exorcist could hardly hear them. The nun, who was in another room, came at the command of the Father, and addressing the Chevalier, first said the indecent words the monk had refused, and then repeated several times *Gloria patri et filio et Spiritui Sancta.* She was ordered to say the words, exactly as she had been desired, but she said she would not.

The Bishop of Nîmes, being present at an exorcism by Father Surin, begged him to order something in difficult Latin; and the Demon thereupon performed what was wanted.

A Jesuit wishing to try what so many people stated they had experienced, gave an inward order to a demon who had been exorcised; and then immediately another. In the space of a second he gave five or six orders, which he countermanded one after another; and thus tormented the Devil, who was ordered to obey his intentions. The Demon repeated his commands aloud, beginning by the first, and adding, "But you wont," and when he had come to the last he said, "Now let's see whether we can do this."

"When it rained," says Father Surin, "the Devil used to place the Mother Superior under the wafer spout. As I knew this to be a habit of his, I commanded him mentally to bring her to me; whereupon she used to come and ask me: 'What do you want.'"

Another thing which struck the Exorcists, was the instantaneous answers they gave to the most difficult questions of Theology, as to grace, the vision of God, Angels, the Incarnation and similar subjects, always in the very terns used in the schools.

The corporal effect of possession is a proof which strikes the coarsest minds. It has this other advantage, that an example convinces a wholeassembly .[11]

Now the nuns of Loudun gave these proofs daily. When the Exorcist gave some order to the Devil, the nuns suddenly passed from a state of quiet into the most terrible convulsions, and without the slightest increase of pulsation. They struck their chests and backs with their heads, as if they had had their neck broken, and with inconceivable rapidity; they twisted their arms at the joints of the shoulder, the elbow and the wrist two or three times round; lying on their stomachs they joined their palms of their hands to the soles of their feet; their faces became so as the commissioners should incline. It further frightful one could not bear to look at them; their eyes remained open without winking; their tongues issued suddenly from their mouths, horribly swollen, black, hard, and covered with pimples, and yet while in this state they spoke distinctly; they threw themselves back till their heads touched their feet, and walked in this position with wonderful rapidity, and for a long time. They uttered: cries so horrible and so loud that nothing like it was ever heard before; they made use of expressions so indecent as to shame the most debauched of men, while their acts, both in exposing themselves and inviting lewd behaviour from those present, would have astonished the inmates of the lowest brothel in the country; they uttered maledictions against the three Divine Persons of the Trinity, oaths and blasphemous expressions so execrable, so unheard of, that they could not have suggested themselves to the human mind. They used to watch without rest, and fast five or six days at a time, or be tortured twice a day as we have described during several hours, without their health suffering; on the contrary, those that were somewhat delicate, appeared healthier than before their possession.

The Devil sometimes made them fall suddenly asleep: they fell to the ground and became so heavy, that the strongest man had great trouble in even moving their heads. Françoise Filestreau having her mouth closed, one could hear within her body different voices speaking at the same time, quarrelling, and discussing who should make her speak.

Lastly, one often saw Elizabeth Blanchard, in her convulsions, with her feet in the air and her head on the ground, leaning against a chair or a window sill without other support.

The Mother Superior from the beginning was carried off her feet and remained suspended in the air at the height of 24 inches. A report of this was drawn up and sent to the Sorbonne, signed by a great number of witnesses, ecclesiastics and doctors, and the judgement thereon of the Bishop of Poitiers who was also a witness. The doctors of the Sorbonne were of the same opinion as the Bishop, and declared that infernal possession was proved.

Both she and other nuns lying flat, without moving foot, hand, or body, were suddenly lifted to their feet like statues. In another exorcism the Mother Superior was suspended in the air, only touching the ground with her elbow.

Others, when comatose, became supple like a thin piece of lead, so that their body could be bent in every direction, forward, backward, or sideways, till their head touched the ground; and they remained thus so long as their position was not altered by others. At other times they passed the left foot over their shoulder to the cheek. They passed also their feet over their head till the big toe touched the tip of the nose.

Others again were able to stretch their legs so far to the right and left that they sat on the ground without any space being visible between their bodies and the floor, their bodies erect and their hands joined. One, the Mother Superior, stretched her legs to such an extraordinary extent, that from toe to toe the distance was 7 feet, though she was herself but 4 feet high. But sometime before the death of Grandier, this lady had a still stranger experience. In a few words this is what happened: In an exorcism the Devil promised Father Lactance as a sign of his exit, that he would make three wounds on the left side of the Mother Superior. He described their appearance and stated the day and hour when they would appear. He said he would come out from within, without affecting the nun's health, and forbade that any remedy should be applied, as the wounds would leave no mark.

On the day named, the exorcism took place; and as many doctors had come from the neighbouring towns to be present at this event, M. de Laubardemont made them draw near, and permitted then to examine the clothes of the nun, to uncover her side in the presence of the assembly, to look into all the folds of her dress, of her stays which were of whalebone, and of her chemise, to make sure there was no weapon: she only had about her her scissors, which were given over to another. M. de Laubardemont asked the doctors to tie her; hut they begged him to let them first see the convulsions they had heard spoken of. He granted this, and during the convulsions the Superior suddenly came to herself with a sigh, pressed her right hand to her left side and withdrew it covered with blood. She was again examined, and the doctors with the whole assembly saw three bloody wounds, of the size stated by the Devil; the chemise, the stays, and the dress were pierced in three places, the largest hole looking as if a pistol bullet had passed through. The nun was thereupon entirely stripped, but no instrument of any description was found upon her. A report was immediately drawn up, and *Monsieur*, brother of the King, who witnessed the facts, with all the nobles of his Court, attested the document.

PART3

ON Friday the 23rd of June, 1634, about three o'clock in the afternoon, the Bishop of Poitiers and M. de Laubardemont being present, Grandier was brought from his prison to the Church of Ste. Croix in his parish, to be present at the exorcisms. All the possessed were there likewise. And as the accused and his partisans declared that the possessions were mere impostures, he was ordered to be himself the exorcist, and the stole was presented to him. He could not refuse, and therefore, taking the stole and the ritual, he received the pastoral benediction, and after the *Veni Creator* had been sung, commenced the exorcism in the usual form. But where he should haughtily have given commands to the demon, instead of saying *Impero*, I command, he said, *Cogor vos*, that is, I am constrained by you. The Bishop sharply reprimanded him, and as he had said that some of the possessed understood Latin, he was allowed to interrogate in Greek. At the same time, the demon cried out by the mouth of Sister Clara: "Eh! speak Greek, or any language you like; I will answer." At these words, he became confused, and could not say anything more.

To behave thus, or to acknowledge the truth of the accusation, is one and the same thing, but other circumstances strengthened this certainty.

Any man whose own writing testifies against him is lost. Now this is what Grandier experienced. The devils, in several instances, confessed four pacts he had entered into.

This word, Pact, is somewhat equivocal. It may mean either the document by which a man gives himself to the devil, or the physical symbols, whose application will produce some particular effects in consequence of the pact. Here is an example of each case. Grandier's pact, or magical characters, whereby he gave himself to Beelzebub, was as follows:—"My Lord and Master, Lucifer, I recognise you as my God, and promise to serve you all my life. I renounce every other God, Jesus Christ, and all other Saints; the Catholic, Apostolic and Roman Church, its Sacraments, with all prayers that may be said for me; and I promise to do all the evil I can. I renounce the holy oil and the water of baptism, together with all the merits of Jesus Christ and his Saints; and should I fail to serve and adore you, and do homage to you thrice daily, I abandon to you my life as your due."

These characters were recognised as being in Grandier's own hand.

Now here is a specimen of the other kind of pact or magical charm. It was composed of the flesh of a child's heart, extracted in an assembly of magicians held at Orleans in 1631, of the ashes of a holy wafer that had been burnt, and of something else which the least straight-laced decency forbids me to name.

A most convincing proof of Grandier's guilt is that one of the devils declared he had marked him in two parts of his body. His eyes were bandaged and he was examined by eight doctors, who reported they had found two marks in each place; that they had inserted a needle to the depth of an inch without the criminal having felt it, and that no blood had been drawn. Now this is a roost decisive test. For however deeply a needle be buried in such marks no pain is caused, and no blood can be extracted when they are magical signs.

But if the devils, overcome by the exorcisms, at times gave evidence against the criminal, at others they seemed to conspire to blacken him still more under the semblance of an apparent justification. Thus several of the possessed spoke in his favour: and some even went so far as to confess that they had calumniated him. Indeed, the Mother Superior herself, one day when M. de Laubardemont was in the convent, stripped herself to her shift, and, with a rope round her neck and a candle in her hand, stood for two hours in the middle of the yard, although it was raining heavily; and when the door of the room in which M. de Laubardemont was seated, was opened, she threw herself on her knees before him, declaring she repented of the crime she had committed in accusing Grandier, who was innocent. She then withdrew and fastened the rope to a tree in the garden, attempting to hang herself, but was prevented by the other nuns.

When the devil played these kind of tricks they forced him to retract, by calling on him to take Jesus Christ present in the Eucharist as witness of the truth of his statement, which he never dared to do.

What criminals could ever be condemned if such proofs were not deemed sufficient? The certainty of the possessions; the depositions of two priests who accused him of sacrilege; those of the nuns, declaring that they saw him day and night for four months, though the gates of the convent were kept locked; the two women who bore witness that he offered to make one of them Princess of the Magicians; the evidence of sixty other witnesses; his own embarrassment and confusion on so many occasions; the disappearance of his three brothers, who had fled and were never seen again; his pact and the magic characters that were afterwards burnt with him: all these placed his guilt beyond doubt.

The trial being completed, and the magician duly convicted, there only remained to sentence the evil doer. The Commissioners assembled at the Carmelite Convent, and it was noticed that there was not the slightest difference of opinion among all the fourteen judges, though they had never seen or known one another. They were all agreed as to the penalty to be inflicted, and having pronounced their sentence, they were filled with joy and their conscience was perfectly at rest. It was as if God, whose honour was so interested in this affair, had intended to give them this consolation.

No one among the Catholics, or, indeed, among all honest men, failed to applaud the sentence on Grandier. It was as follows:—

"We have declared, and declare the said Urbain Grandier attainted and convicted of the crimes of magic, maleficence and possession occurring through his act, in the persons of certain Ursuline Nuns of this town of Loudun, and other women; together with other crimes resulting therefrom. For reparation whereof we have condemned, and do condemn, the said Grandier to make 'amende honorable' bareheaded, a rope round his neck, holding in his hand a burning torch of the weight of two pounds, before the principal gate of Saint Pierre du Marché, and before that of Saint Ursula of the said town; and there, on his knees, to ask pardon of God, the King, and Justice, and that done, to be led to the public square of Sainte Croix, to be there tied to a stake, which for that purpose shall be erected in the said square, and his body to be there burnt with the pacts and magical inscriptions now in custody of the Court, together with the manuscript book written by him against the celibacy of priests, and his ashes to be scattered to the wind. We have declared all his property forfeited and confiscated to the Crown, less a sum of 150 livres, which shall be expended in the purchase of a copper plate, on which shall be engraved the present sentence, and the same shall be placed in a prominent position in the said Church of St. Ursula, there to be preserved for ever. And before this present sentence shall be carried out, we order that the said Grandier shall be put to the question ordinary and extraordinary, to discover his accomplices.—

Pronounced at Loudun on the said Grandier, and executed the 18th of August, 1634."

In execution of this sentence, he was taken to the Court of Justice of Loudun. His sentence having been read to him, he earnestly begged M. de Laubardemont and the other Commissioners to mitigate the rigour of their sentence. M. de Laubardemont replied that the only means of inducing the judges to moderate the penalties was to declare at once his accomplices, and by some act of repentance for his past crimes to implore Divine mercy. The only answer he gave was, that he had no accomplices, which was false; for there is no magician but must be accompanied by others.

For the last forty days the Commissioner had placed at his side two monks to convert him. But all was in vain. Nothing could touch this hardened sinner. It is true, however, that the conversion of a magician is so rare an occurrence that it must be placed in the rank of miracles. "I am not astonished," says one who was present, "at his impenitence, nor at his refusing to acknowledge himself guilty of magic, both under torture and at his execution, for it is known that magicians promise the devil never to confess this crime, and he in return hardens their heart, so that they go to their death stupid and altogether insensible to their misfortunes." Before being put to the torture, the prisoner was addressed by Father Lactance, a man of great faith, chosen by the Bishop of Poitiers to exorcise the instruments of torture, as is always done in the case of magicians, in order to induce him to repent. Every one shed tears except the prisoner. M. de Laubardemont also spoke to him, together with the Lieutenant Criminel of Orleans, but, notwithstanding their efforts, they made no impression. This determined M. de Laubardemont to try the effects of torture. The boots[12] were applied, and the judge repeated his questions as to his accomplices. He always replied that he was no magician; though he had committed greater crimes than that. Questioned as to what crimes, he replied, crimes of human frailty, and added, that were he guilty of magic, he would be less ashamed of that than of his other crimes. This speech was ridiculous, especially in the mouth of a priest, who must know better than a layman that of all crimes the greatest is that of sorcery.

Torture drew from him nothing but cries, or rather sighs from the depth of his bosom, unaccompanied by tears, though the exorcist had abjured him, according to the ritual, to weep if he were innocent, but if guilty to remain tearless. Though he was very thirsty, he several times refused to drink holy water when presented to him. At length, pressed to drink, he took a. few drops, with glaring eyes and a horrible look on his face. Never in the greatest agony of torture did he mention the name of Jesus Christ or of the Holy Virgin, save when repeating words he was ordered to speak, and then only in so cold a manner, and with such constraint, that he horrified the assistants. He never cast his eyes on the image of Christ, nor on that of the Virgin, which were opposite to him, and they were offered to ban in vain: whereupon the judges remonstrated with him. They were still more scandalised when they tried to make him say the prayer which every good Christian addresses to his guardian angel, especially in great extremities, and he said he did not know it. Such was his conduct under torture: in such a crisis every feeling of religion would be awakened in an ordinary man.

His legs were then washed and placed near the fire to restore circulation; he then began to talk to the guards, joking and laughing, and would have gone on had they allowed him. He spoke neither of receiving the sacrament of penitence nor of imploring God's pardon.

They had given him for a confessor Father Archangel, who asked him if he did not wish to confess. He replied that he had done so the previous Tuesday, after which he sat down and dined with the same appetite as usual, drank three or four glasses of wine, and spoke of all kinds of things except of God. Instead of listening to what was said to him for the good of his soul, he made speeches he had prepared beforehand as if he were preaching. They consisted in complaints as to the pain in his legs, and of a feeling of chilliness about his head, in asking for something to drink or to eat, and in begging that he might not be burnt alive.

When he was carried to the Court-house, where the Holy Fathers began to prepare him for death, he pushed back with his hand a crucifix which was presented to him, and muttered between his teeth some words which were not heard. His guards, witnessing this action, were scandalised, and told the monk not to offer him the crucifix again since he rejected it. He recommended himself to no one's prayers, neither before nor during the execution of the sentence–only, as he passed through the streets, turning his head on one side and the other to see the people, it was noticed that he said twice, with an appearance of vanity, "Pray God for me," and that those to whom he spoke were Huguenots, among whom was an Apostate. The monk who was with him exhorted him to say, "Cor mundum crea in me, Deus." Grandier turned his back on him and said with contempt, "Cor mundum crea in me, Deus."

Having reached the place of execution, the fathers redoubled their charitable solicitude, and pressed him most earnestly to be converted to God at that moment, offered him the crucifix, and placed it over his mouth and on his chest, he never deigned to look at it, and once or twice even turned away; he shook his head when holy water was offered him. He seemed eager to end his days, and in haste to have the fire lighted, either because he expected not to feel it, or because he feared he might be weak enough to name his accomplices; or perhaps, as is believed, in fear lest pain should extract from him a renunciation of his master Lucifer. For the devil, to whom magicians give themselves body and soul, so thoroughly masters their mind that they fear him only, and expect and hope for nothing save from him. Therefore did Grandier protest, placing his hand on his heart that he would say no more than he had already said. At last, seeing them set fire to the faggots, he feared they did not intend to keep their promise to him, but wished to burn him alive, and uttered loud complaints-The executioner then advanced, as is always done, to strangle him; but the flames suddenly sprang up with such violence that the rope caught fire, and he fell alive among the burning faggots. Just before this a strange event happened. In the midst of this mass of people, notwithstanding the noise of so many voices and the efforts of the archers who shook their halberts in the air to frighten them, a flight of pigeons flew round and round the stake. Grandier's partisans, impudent to the end, said that these innocent birds came, in default of men, as witnesses of his innocence; others thought very differently, and said that it was a troop of demons who came, as sometimes happens on the death of great magicians, to assist at that of Grandier, whose scandalous impenitence certainly deserved to be honoured in this manner. His friends, however, called this hardness of heart constancy, and had his ashes collected as if they were relics, they who did not believe in such things, for the Huguenots looked upon him as one of themselves, especially when they noticed that he never called on the Virgin nor looked on the crucifix.

Thus did he close his criminal career by a death which horrified not only Catholics, but even the more honourable of the Calvinist party.

But the end of the magician was not the end of the effects of his sorcery; and the possessions, far from ceasing, as had been hoped, continued for a time. God permitted that a great number of those who had been connected with the affair should be more or less vexed by demons. The Civil Lieutenant, Louis Chauvet, was seized with such fear-that his mind gave way, and he never recovered. The Sieur Mannouri, the Surgeon who had sounded the marks[13] which the devil had impressed on the magician priest, suffering from extraordinary troubles, was of course said by the friends of Grandier to be the victim of remorse. Here are the particulars of the death of this Surgeon—

One night as he was returning about ten o'clock from visiting a sick man, walking with a friend, and accompanied by a man carrying a lantern, he cried all of a sudden, like a man awaking from a dream, "Ah! there is Grandier! what do you want?" At the same time he was seized with trembling. The two men took him back to his home, while he continued to talk to Grandier whom he thought he had before his eyes. He was put to bed filled with the same illusion, and shaking in every limb. He only lived a few days, during which his state never changed. He died believing the magician was still before him, and making efforts to keep him at arm's length.

Father Lactance, the worthy monk who had assisted the possessed in their sufferings, was himself attacked some time after the death of the priest. Feeling the first symptoms, he determined to go to Notre Dame des Ardilliers, whose chapel served by the priests of the oratory is held in great veneration in Saumur and its neighbourhood. M. de Canaye, who was going into the country, gave him a seat in his carriage. He had heard speak of his state, and knew that he was tormented by the devil, but he nevertheless joked about the matter, when, all of a sudden, whilst rolling along a perfectly level road, the carriage turned over with the wheels in the air without any one being in any way hurt. The next day they continued their voyage to Saumur when the carriage again turned over in the same way in the middle of the Rue du Faubourg de Fenet, which is perfectly smooth, and leads to the chapel of Ardillier. This holy monk afterwards experienced the greatest vexations from the demons, who at times deprived him of sight, and at times of memory; they produced in him violent fits of nausea, dulled his intelligence, and worried him in numerous ways. At length, after being tried by so many evils, God called him to Him.

Five years later, died of the same disease Father Tranquille. He was a holy monk, a celebrated preacher, gifted with a judicious mind, great piety, and a profound humility. A laborious exorcist, much feared by the devils, he had preferred that painful duty, generally little sought for, to the fame of preaching, and had devoted himself to the service of the possessed of Loudun. The demons, irritated at his constancy, determined to possess his body. But God never allowed him to be entirely possessed. Nevertheless, his cruel enemies succeeded in attacking his senses to a certain extent. They cast him to the ground, they cursed and swore out of his mouth, they caused him to put out his tongue and hiss like a serpent, they filled his mind with darkness, seemed to crush out his heart, and overwhelmed him with a thousand other torments.

On the day of Pentecoast they attacked bins more violently than ever, Ile was to have preached, but was too ill to attempt it. But his confessor ordered the devil to leave him at liberty, and commanded the father to ascend the pulpit. He did so, and preached more eloquently than if he had prepared his sermon for weeks. This was his last sermon.

He performed mass for two or three days more, and then took to his bed to rise no more. The demons caused him pains, the violence of which none knew but he; they shrieked and howled out of his mouth, but he remained clear headed. The following morning the monks saw that God had given rein to the powers of hell, and had determined to abandon to them the life of the monk; and he himself begged that Extreme Unction should be administered to him when they should see that he was passing away. About twelve o'clock a demon who was being exorcised declared that Father Tranquille was at his last gasp. They hastened to see if it were true; be was dying, so the sacrament was administered to him. He died, and received the crown he had gained by combats with hell so courageously sustained.

The opinion of his holiness attracted an enormous crowd to his funeral. A Jesuit pronounced his funeral elogy, and a worthy epitaph was engraved on his tomb.

Another matter that should be mentioned is that when, Extreme Unction was administered to him, the devils, driven away by the sacrament, were forced to leave him. But they did not go far; for they entered the body of another excellent monk who was present, and whom they possessed henceforward. They vexed him at first by violent contortions and horrible howlings, and at the moment of Tranquille's death they cried horribly, "He is dead;" as if they would say, "It is all over, no more hope of this soul!" At the same time, casting themselves on the other monk, they worked him so horribly that, in spite of the many that held him, he kept kicking in the most violent manner towards the deceased. He had to be carried away.

Father Surin, a Jesuit, had succeeded Father Lactance; he too had his trials.

The demons used to threaten him out of the mouth of the Mother Superior, who was under his care. Once, in the presence of the Bishop of Nimes, the demon took up his position on the face of the nun; suddenly he disappeared and attacked the father, made him grow pale, sat on his chest, and stopped his voice; but soon, obeying the order of another exorcist, he returned to the nun, spoke through her mouth, and showed himself extremely hideous and horrible on her face; and the father, returning to the fight, continued his duties as if he had never been attacked. In one afternoon he was thus attacked and released seven or eight times; but these assaults were followed by others still more violent, so that in his exorcisms he seemed to be struck with violent interior blows, borne to earth, and violently shaken by his adversary; he remained in this state sometimes half an hour, sometimes an hour. The other exorcists applied the Holy Sacrament to the places where he felt the demons, sometimes to his chest, sometimes to his head. When the devil left him he reappeared on the face of the mother, where the monk, with holy vengeance, pursued him, and constrained him to adore the Holy Sacrament. Once the devil threw him out of a window on to the rock where stands the convent of the Jesuits, and broke one of his thighs. After having sustained during many years with perfect patience and resignation these terrible trials, he was freed from them, and at length died in the odour of sanctity.

As to the Mother Superior, towards the end of the year 1635, something happened to her of a most extraordinary nature. Lord Montague came to Loudun, accompanied by two other English noblemen. He brought the exorcists a letter from the Archbishop of Tours, ordering them to edify his Lordship as much as possible. The Superior, in the `midst of a convulsion, stretched out her left arm, and the name of Joseph appeared on it written in capital letters. The report of this event was signed by the English noblemen. Lord Montague hastened to Rome, abjured his heresy, embraced the ecclesiastical career, and, under another name, settled in France, where he lived many years. He is mentioned in the memoirs of Madame de Motteville.

At the beginning of 1636, on Twelfth Night, Father Surin resolved to compel the last demon that remained in the Mother Superior to adore Jesus Christ. He had the lady tied to a bench. The exorcisms drove the demon into a fury; and instead of obeying, he vomited a multitude of maledictions and blasphemies against the three persons of the Holy Trinity, against Jesus Christ, and against his Holy Mother, so execrable that one would he horrified to read them. The father knew that he was about to come out, and had the lady unbound. After tremblings, contortions, and horrible howlings, Father Surin pressed him more and more with the Holy Sacrament in his hand, and ordered him in Latin to write the name of Mary on the lady's hand. Raising her left arm into the air, the fiend redoubled his cries and howls, and in a last convulsion issued from the lady, leaving on her hand the holy name Maria, in letters so perfectly formed that no human hand could imitate them. The lady felt herself free and full of joy; and a *TeDeum* was sung in honour of the e vent.

Such is the true story of the possession of the nuns of Loudun and of the condemnation of Urbain Grandier, so different from the false accounts hitherto published. Even those who do not blush to deny the truth of infernal possessions need only notice that the human race has always believed, and still believes, that there are intelligent creatures in existence other than man, and almost similar to those whom the Pagans have always represented as Gods of Evil, or subterranean genii, like the demons believed in by Christians; and the belief in infernal possession, having in it no longer anything repugnant, will seem at once to them not only possible but probable. To believe that Urbain Grandier was unjustly condemned and executed, we must blindly believe hundreds of things which revolt common sense. One of the Protestant writers, for example, after having said in a thousand different ways that the possession of the nuns of Loudun was a mere imposture and horrible farce, confesses that it is impossible to conceive human beings, and especially women, driving a priest to a horrible death by such a series of feigned possessions.

APPENDIX 1

Instances sent me (Baxter) from the Duke of Lauderdale; more in other Letters of his I gave away, and some Books of Forreign Wonders he sent me.

Sir,

It is sad that the Sadducean, or rather atheistical denying of spirits, or their apparitions, should so far prevail; and sadder, that the clear testimonies of so many ancient and modern authors should not convince them. But why should I wonder, if those who believe not Moses and the prophets, will not believe though one should rise from the dead? One great cause of the hardening of these infidels is, the frequent impostures which the Romanists obtrude on the world in their exorcisms and pretended miracles. Another is the too great credulity of some who make everything witchcraft which they do not understand; and a third may be the ignorance of some judges and juries, who condemn silly melancholy people upon their own confession, and perhaps slender proofs. None of these three can be denied, but it is impertinent arguing to conclude, that because there have been cheats in the world, because there are some too credulous, and some have been put to death for witches, and were not, therefore all men are deceived. There is so much written, both at home and abroad, so convincingly, and by so unquestionable authors, that I have not the vanity to add any thing, especially to you; but because you have desired me to tell you the story of the nuns at Loudun, and some others, I shall first tell you of a real possession near the place I was born in; next of disquietings by spirits, (both of which I had from unquestionable testimonies) and then I shall tell you what I saw at Loudun, concerning that which I do not doubt to call a pretended possession, sure I am a cheat. About 30 years ago, when I was a boy at school, there was a poor woman generally believed to be really possessed. She lived near the town of Duns, in the Mers, and Mr John Weems, then minister of Duns, (a man known by his works to be a learned man, and I knew him to be a godly honest man,) was perswaded she was possessed. I have heard him many times speak with my father about it, and both of them concluded it a real possession. Mr Weems visited her often, and being convinced of the truth of the thing, he, with some, neighbour ministers, applied themselves to the king's privy council for a warrant to keep days of humiliation for her; but the bishops being then in power, would not allow any fasts to be kept. I will not trouble you with many circumstances; one I shall only tell you, which I think will evince a real possession. The report being spread in the country, a knight of the name of Forbes, who lived in the north of Scotland, being come to Edinborough, meeting there with a minister of the north, and both of them desirous to see the woman, the northern minister invited the knight to my father's house, (which was within ten or twelve miles of the woman) whither they came, and next morning went to see the woman. They found her a poor ignorant creature, and seeing nothing extraordinary, the minister says in Latin to the knight, to *"Nondum audivimus spiritum loquentem."* Presently a voice comes out of the woman's mouth, *"Audi, loquentem, audis loquentem."* This put the minister into some amazement, (which I think made him not mind his own Latin,) he took off his hat, and said, *"Misereatur Deus pectatoris;"* the voice presently out of the woman's mouth said, *"Dic peccatricis, dic peccatricis;"* whereupon both of them came out of the house fully satisfied, took horse immediately, and returned to my father's house at Thirlestoane Castle, in Lauderdale, where they related this passage. This I do exactly remember. Many more particulars might be got in that country, but this Latin criticism, in a most illiterate ignorant woman, where there was no pretence to dispossessing, is evidence enough, I think.

Within these 30 or 40 years, there was an unquestionable possession in the United Provinces; a wench that spoke all the languages, of which I have heard many particulars when I lived in the Low Countries. But that being forreign, I will not insist on it.

As to houses disquieted with noises, I shall tell you one that happened since I was a married man, and hint at more, which, if you please, I can get you authentically attested.

Within four miles of Edinborough, there lived an aged godly minister, one that was esteemed a Puritan; his son, now minister of the same place, and then ordained his assistant. Their house was extraordinarily troubled with noises, which they and their family, and many neighbours (who for divers weeks used to go watch with them) did ordinarily hear. It troubled them most on the Saturday night, and the night before their weekly lecture day. Sometimes they would hear all the locks in the house, on doors and chests, to fly open; yea, their cloaths, which were at night locked up into trunks and chests, they found in the morning all hanging about the walls. Once they found their best linnen taken out, the table covered with it, napkins as if they had been used, yea, and liquor in their cups as if company had been there at meat. The rumbling was extraordinary; the good old man commonly called his family to prayer when it was most troublesome, and immediately it was converted into gentle knocking, like the modest knock of a finger; but as soon as prayer was done, they should hear excessive knocking, as if a beam had been heaved by strength of many men against the floor.

Never was there voice or apparition; but one thing was remarkable (you must know that it is ordinary in Scotland to have a half cannon-bullet in the chimney-corner, on which they break their great coals,) a merry maid in the house, being accustomed to the rumblings, and so her fear gone, told her fellow maid-servant that if the devil troubled them that night, she would brain him, so she took the half cannon-bullet into bed; the noise did not fail to awake her, nor did she fail in her design, but took up the great bullet, and with a threatning, threw it, as she thought, on the floor, but the bullet was never more seen; the minister turned her away for meddling and talking to it. Alt these particulars I have had from the mouth of the minister, now living; he is an honest man, of good natural parts, well bred both in learning and by travel into foreign parts in his youth. I was not in the country myself during the time, but I have it from many other witnesses; and my father's steward lived then in a house of mine, within a mile of the place, and sent his servants constantly thither; his son now serves me, who knows it.

I could tell you an ancienter story before my time, in the house of one Burnet, in the north of Scotland, where strange things were seen, which I can get sufficiently attested, Also in the southwest border of Scotland, in Annandale, there is a house called Powdine, belonging to a gentleman called Johnston; that house hath been haunted these 50 or 60 years. At my coming to Worcester, 1651, I spoke with the gentleman, (being myself quartered within two miles of the house,) he told me many extraordinary relations consisting in his own knowledge; and I carried him to my master, to whom he made the same relations,—noises and apparitions, drums and trumpets heard before the last war, yea, he said that some English soldiers quartered in his house were soundly beaten by that irresistible inhabitant; (this last I wondered at, for 1 rather expected he should have been a remonstrater, and opposed the resistance,) and within this fortnight Mr. James Sharp was with me, (him you know, and he is now at London,) he tells me that spirit now speaks, and appears frequently in the shape of a naked arm; but other discourses took me off from further inquiry. These things I tell you in obedience to your desire, hut as I said before, I desire them not to be printed. Atheists are not to be convinced by stories; their own senses will no more convert them than sense will convert a papist from transubstantiation; and Scottish stories would make the disaffected jeer Scotland, which is the object of acorn enough already.

When I was in Dorsetshire, prisoner, one Mr Jo. Hodder, minister of Hauke-church, in that county, told me of strange apparitions and unquestionable evidences of the actings of spirits in a house, yea, a religious house of that county, of which he was himself an ear and eye-witness.

In Dorchester also, the son of a Reverend Mr Jo. White, (who was assessor to the Assembly at Westminster,) told me many particulars of that house in Lambeth, where his father lived in the time of the Assembly, which then was unquestionably haunted with spirits. I do well remember I dined with old Mr White there one day, and at dinner he told me much of it; and that that morning the spirit called up the maid to lay the beef to the fire. Of the two last you may be satisfied when you please: and at this present I am told that there is a house at Folie-John-Park, not three miles from the place, haunted with spirits.

But I must leave room for my Loudun nuns, and not write a book. In the year 1637, being at Paris in the spring, the city was so full of the possession of a whole cloyster of nuns, and some laick wenches at Loudun, books printed, and strange stories told, that few doubted it; and I, who was perswaded such a thing might be, and that it was not impossible the devil could possess a nun as well as another, doubted it as little as any body.

So coming into that country, I went a day's journey out of my way to satisfy my curiosity. Into the chappel I came in the morning of a holy day, and with as little prejudice as any could have, for I believed verily to have seen some strange sights; but when I had seen exorcising enough of three or four of them in the chappel, and could hear nothing but wanton wenches singing bandy songs in French, I began to suspect a fourbe, and in great gravity went to a jesuite, and told him I had come a great way in hope to see some strange thing, and was sorry to be disappointed. He commended my holy curiosity, and after he had thought a while, he desired me to go to the Castle, and from thence, at such an hour, to the parish church, and I should be satisfied. I wondered at his correspondence, yet gravely went where he directed me. In the Castle I saw little, but in the parish church I saw a great many people gazing, and a wench pretty well taught to play tricks, yet nothing so much as I have seen twenty tumblers and rope-dancers do. Back I came to the nuns chappel, where I saw the jesuits still hard at work, at several altars, and one poor capuchin, who was an object of pity, for he was possessed indeed with a melancholy fancy that devils were running about his head, and constantly was applying relicks. I saw the mother superior exorcised, and saw the hand on which they would have made us believe the names I. H. S. Maria Joseph were written by miracles; (but it was apparent to me it was done with aquafortis) then my patience was quite spent, and I went to a jesuit and told him my mind freely. He still maintained a real possession, and I desired for a tryal, to speak a strange language. He asked, "What language?" I told him, "I would not tell; but neither he nor all those devils should understand me."

He asked, "If I would be converted upon the tryal?" (for I had discovered I was no papist.) I told him, "That was not the question, nor could all the devils in hell pervert me i but the question was, if that was a real possession, and if any could understand me, I shall confess it under my hand." His answer was, "These devils have not travelled;" and this I replied to with a loud laughter, nor could I get any more satisfaction; only in the town I heard enough that it was a cheat invented to burn a curate, (his name, as I take it, was Cupiff,) and the man had been really burned to ashes as a witch, but the people said it was for his conversion from them. At my coming to Saumar next day, my countryman, Dr, Duncan, Principle of the College at Saumar, told me how he had made a clearer discovery of the cheat in presence of the Bishop of Poitiers, and of all the country, how he had held fast one of the pretended nuns arms, in spite of all the power of their exorcisms, and challenged all the devils in hell to take it out of his hand. This, with many more circumstances, he told me, and he printed them to the world; but this is already too tedious.

One more journey I made to see possessed women exorcised near Antwerp, anno 16493 but saw only some great Holland wenches hear exorcism patiently, and belch most abominably. So if those were devils, they were windy devils, but I thought they were only possessed with a morning's draught of too new beer. Some of the Loudun nuns, after great resistance and squeaking, did, on great importunity, adore their host, and the jesuites did desire us to see the power of the church, where all I wondered at was his blasphemy, in saying to the pretended devil,—"*Prostratum adorabis creatorem tuum, quem digitis teneo;*" but my paper, as well as my discretion, calls for an end. Your desire, and my obedience, is all I can plead for your receiving so long a rabble, from, Sir,

Your most faithful Friend and Servant,

Lauderdaile.

Windsor Castle, March12, 1659.

APPENDIX 2

[The following Notes are taken from Arnot's Collection of Criminal Trials in Scotland]:—

1588.

Alison Pearson.

Alison Pearson in Byre-hills, Fifeshire,[14] was convicted of practising sorcery, and of invoking the Devil. She confessed that she had associated with the Queen of the Fairies for many years,[15] and that she had friends in the Court of Elfland, who were of her own blood. She said that William Simpson, late the King's smith, was, in the eighth year of his age, carried off by an Egyptian to Egypt, where he remained twelve years; and that this Egyptian was a giant: That the Devil appeared to her in the form of this William Simpson, who was a great scholar, and a doctor of medicine, who cured her diseases: That he has appeared to her, accompanied with many men and women, who made merry with bag-pipes, good cheer, and wine: That the good neighbours[16] attended, and prepared their charms in pans over the fire; that the herbs of which they composed their charms, were gathered before sunrise; and that with these they cured the Bishop of St. Andrews of a fever and flux.—She underwent all the legal forms customary in cases of witchcraft, *i.e.* she was convicted and condemned, strangled and burned.

1590.

Janet Grant and Janet Clerk.

Janet Grant and Janet Clerk[17] were convicted of bewitching several persons to death, of taking away the privy members of some folks, and bestowing them on others; and of raising the devil.

John Cunninghame.

It was proved against John Cunninghame, that the Devil appeared to him in white raiment,[18] and promised, that, if he would become his servant, he should never want, and should be revenged of all his enemies: That he was carried in an ecstacy to the kirk of North Berwick, where the Devil preached to him, and many others, bidding them not spare to do evil, but to eat, drink, and be merry; for he should raise them all up gloriously at the Last Day: That the Devil made him do homage, by kissing his . . . . That he (the prisoner) raised the wind on the King's passage to Denmark: That he met with Satan on the King's return from Denmark; and Satan promised to raise a mist by which his Majesty should be thrown upon the coast of England; and thereupon threw something like a football into the sea, which raised a vapour.

Agnes Sampson.

Agnes Sampson in Keith,[19] a grave matron-like woman, of a rank and comprehension above the vulgar, was accused of having renounced her baptism, and of having received the devil's mark; of raising storms to prevent the Queen's coming from Denmark; of being at the famous meeting at North Berwick, where six men and ninety women, witches, were present, dancing to one of their number, who played to them on a Jew's-harp. It was charged in the indictment that the Devil was present at this meeting; and started up in the pulpit, which was hung round with black candles: That he called them all by their names, asked them, If they had kept their promises, and been good servants, and what they had done since the last meeting: That they opened up three graves, and cut off the joints from the dead bodies fingers, and that the prisoner got for her share two joints and a winding sheet, to make powder of to do mischief: That the Devil was dressed in a black gown and hat; and that he ordered them to keep his commandments, which were to do all the ill they could, and to kiss his . . . .

1591.

Euphan M'Calzeane.

Euphan M'Calzeane was a lady possessed of a considerable estate in her own right. She was the daughter of Thomas M'Calzeane Lord Cliftonhall, one of the Senators of the College of Justice, whose death in the year 1581, spared him the disgrace and misery of seeing his daughter fall by the hands of the executioner. She was married to a gentleman of her own name, by whom she had three children. She was accused of treasonably conspiring the King's death by enchantments;[20] particularly by training a waxen picture of the King; of raising storms to hinder his return from Denmark; and of various other articles of witchcraft. She was heard by counsel in her defence; was found guilty by the jury, which consisted of landed gentlemen of note; and her punishment was still severer than that commonly inflicted on the Weyward Sisters,—She was burned alive, and her estate confiscated. Her children, however, after being thus barbarously robbed of their mother, were[21] restored by act of Parliament against the forfeiture. The act does not say that the sentence was unjust; but that the King was touched in honour and conscience to restore the children. But to move the wheels of his Majesty's conscience, the children had to grease them, by a payment of five thousand merks to the donator of escheat,[22] and by relinquishing the estate of Clifton-hall, which the King gave to Sir James Sandilands of Slamanno.

As a striking picture of the state of justice, humanity, and science in those times,[23] it may be remarked that this Sir James Sandilands, a favourite of the King's, ("ex interiore principis familiaritate,") who got this estate, which the daughter of one Lord of Session forfeited, on account of being a witch, did that very year murder another Lord of Session in the suburbs of Edinburgh, in the public street, without undergoing either trial or punishment.

1620.

Margaret Wallace.

Margaret Wallace[24] was tried before the Court of Justiciary. The Duke of Lennox, the Archbishop of Glasgow, and Sir George Erskine of Innerteil, sat as assessors to the judges, and an eminent counsel was heard in behalf of the prisoner. She was accused of inflicting and of curing diseases by inchantment; but it was not specified what spells she employed. It was libelled against her, that on being taken suddenly ill she sent for one Christian Graham, a notorious witch, who afterwards suffered a capital punishment, and that this witch transferred the disease from the prisoner to a young girl: That the girl being thus taken ill, her mother was advised by the prisoner to send for Christian Graham, who answered, that her confidence was in God, and she would have nothing to do with the Devil or his instruments: The prisoner replied, "That in a case of this sort Christian Graham could do as much as God himself; and that without her aid there was no remedy for the child:" But the mother not consenting, the prisoner without her knowledge sent for

Christian, who muttered words, and expressed signs, by which she restored the child to health, &c. Her counsel urged, that the indictment was much too general: That it ought to have been specified, not simply that she did enchant, but also by what kind of spells she performed her incantations: That supposing Christian Graham to have been a witch, and that the prisoner when taken ill consulted her, still he was entitled to plead that the prisoner consulted her on account of her medical knowledge, and not for her skill in sorcery: That as to blasphemous expressions however well they might found a trial for blasphemy, they by no means inferred the crime of witchcraft; and he quoted many authorities from the Civil and Canon laws. He farther challenged one of the assizers, because one of the articles charged against the prisoner was her having done an injury to his brother-in-law.—The whole defences were repelled by the judges; and the jury found the prisoner guilty.

1629.

Isobel Young.

Isobel Young in East Barns was accused of having stopped by enchantment George Sandie's mill twenty-nine years before; of having prevented his boat from catching fish while all the other boats at the herring, drave, or herring fishery, were successful; and that she was the cause of his failing in his circumstances, and of nothing prospering with him in the world: That she threatened mischief against one Kerse, who thereupon lost the power of his leg and arm: That she entertained several witches in her house, one of whom went out at the roof in likeness of a cat, and then resumed her own shape: That she took a disease off her husband, laid it under the barn floor, and transferred it to his nephew, who when he came into the barn saw the firlot hopping up and down the floor: That she used the following charm to preserve herself and her cattle from an infectious distemper, viz. to bury a white ox and a cat alive throwing in a quantity of salt along with them: That she had the Devil's mark, etc.

Mr Laurence Macgill and Mr David Primrose appeared as counsel for the prisoner. They pleaded, that the mill might have stopped, the boat catched no fish, and the man not prospered in the world, from—natural causes; and it was not libelled by what spells she had accomplished them: That as to the man who had lost the power of his leg and arm, first, she never had the least acquaintance with him; secondly, she offered to prove that he was lame previous to the threatening expressions which she was said to have used: That the charge of laying a disease under a barn floor was a ridiculous fable, taken probably from a similar story in Ariosto; and that two years had elapsed between her husband's illness and his nephew's: That what the prosecutor called the Devil's mark was nothing else than the scar of an old ulcer; and that the charge of her burying the white ox and the cat was false.

The celebrated Sir Thomas Hope, who was counsel for the prosecution, replied, that these defences ought to be repelled, and no proof allowed of them, because contrary to the libel; that is to say, in other words, because what was urged by the prisoner in her defences contradicted what was charged by the public prosecutor in his indictment.—The defences for the prisoner were overruled.—Is it needful for me to add that she was convicted, strangled, and burned?